An Activity Book

Learning about My Baptism

Walnut Springs Press

Cover design by Tracy Anderson (tracyandersonphoto.com)

Illustrations by Molly Cannon Hadfield on cover and on pages 3, 6 (boy), 7, 9–11, 13, 18–20, 22, 24, 29–30, 33–34, 36–37, 39, 43–50, 54, 57–60, 62 (family praying), 65, 67, 71–72, 73 (snowman), 75, 77, 80–81, 87, 105, and 109.

Interior text and illustrations copyright © 2017 by Walnut Springs Press
Interior design copyright © 2017 by Walnut Springs Press
Cover design copyright © 2017 by Walnut Springs Press

ISBN-13: 978-1-59992-201-0

Printed in the United States of America.

What Is a Gospel Principle?

Just as when Jesus Christ was here on the earth, there are certain gospel principles we must learn and obey today. Do you know what a principle is? Trace over the dots in each letter to find out.

A

OR

What Is a Gospel Ordinance?

Now that you know what a gospel principle is, can you guess what a gospel ordinance is? To find the answer, cross out each box with a star in it, then write the leftover letters in the blanks.

A	R	N ☆	I	T
G ☆	E	P ☆	O	R
C	E	R	E	T ☆
M	O	U ☆	N	Y

———   ——— ——— ——— ———   ——— ———

——— ——— ——— ——— ——— ——— ———

What Is a Gospel Rite or Ceremony?

What is a gospel rite or ceremony? To find out, write the words from the circle in the spaces with the same number in the blank circle. Then read the words in clockwise order, starting with "1."

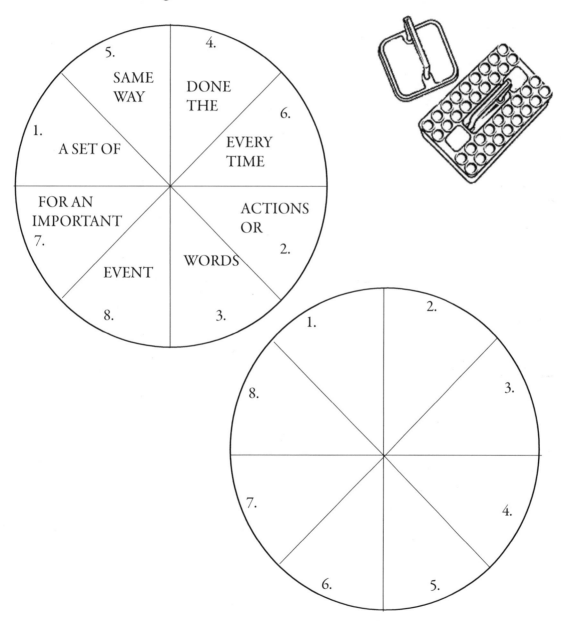

The First Principle of the Gospel

Do you know the first principle of the gospel of Jesus Christ? To find the answer, write the correct letter in the space with the same shape as that letter.

The Meaning of Faith

What does it mean to have faith? The vowels are missing from some of the words below. Write the missing vowels in the correct blanks. Then read the completed sentence to find out what it means to have faith.

E E E E O O U

To have faith is to h__p__

for things which are n__t

s__ __n which are tr__ __.

The Second Principle of the Gospel

What is the second principle of the gospel of Jesus Christ? To find the answer, find your way through the maze and write each letter that crosses your path in order at the bottom of the page. Hint: There is only ONE correct way through the maze.

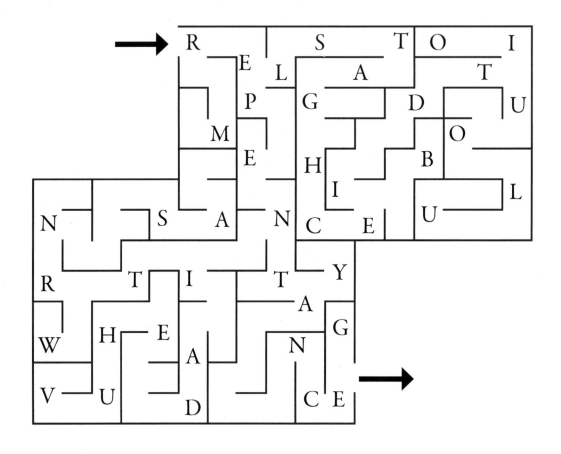

The Third Principle and Ordinance of the Gospel

The third principle and ordinance of the gospel of Jesus Christ is one of the most important steps we can take in our lives. Do you know what this principle is? To find out, write the first letter of each picture in the space below it.

· · · · · · · · · · · · · · · · · · ·						

The Fourth Principle and Ordinance of the Gospel

The fourth principle and ordinance of the gospel is the gift of the Holy Ghost. How do we receive this gift? To find out, cross out every letter that is in the square four times. Then, starting in the first row of blanks, write the leftover letters in order.

Q	L	C	A	Y	B	Z
I	N	Q	G	O	Z	N
P	B	O	Q	C	F	Z
H	Z	P	A	N	B	C
Q	D	B	C	P	S	P

_ _ _ _ _ _ _ _   _ _   _ _

_ _ _ _ _

An Article of Faith

Do you know which Article of Faith talks about the first four principles and ordinances of the gospel? To find out, color all of the boxes that have an F.

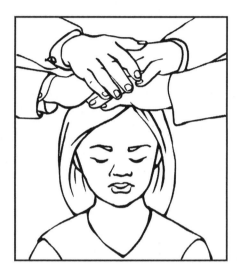

THE

O	O	O	O	O	O	O	O	O	O	O	O	O
O	F	R	F	R	R	F	R	R	F	R	R	O
O	F	R	F	R	F	F	F	R	F	F	F	O
O	F	R	F	R	R	F	R	R	F	R	F	O
O	F	F	F	R	R	F	F	R	F	R	F	O
O	U	U	F	U	U	U	U	U	U	U	U	O
O	U	U	F	U	U	U	U	U	U	U	U	O
O	U	U	F	U	U	U	U	U	U	U	U	O
O	O	O	O	O	O	O	O	O	O	O	O	O

ARTICLE OF FAITH

The Fourth Article of Faith

Finish the fourth Article of Faith by filling in each space with the letter that has the same number.

A=1 D=2 E=3 F=4 I=5 L=6 N=7 O=8 P=9 R=10 S=11 T=12

"WE BELIEVE THAT THE ____ ____ ____ ____ ____
                      4   5   10   11   12

PRINCIPLES AND ORDINANCES OF THE

G ____ ____ P____ ____ ARE: FIRST, F ____ ____ TH IN
  8   11   3   6   1   5

THE L___ ___ ___ JESUS CHRIST; SECOND,
    8   10 2

REPE___ ___ ___ .___CE; THIRD, B___ ___ ___ISM BY
    7   12 1   7   1   9   12

IMMERSION FOR THE REMISSION

OF S___ ___S; FOURTH, LAYING ON OF HANDS FOR
   5   7

THE G___ ___T OF THE HOLY GHOST."
    5   4

A Baptism Story: The Prophet Joseph Smith

One day while Joseph Smith and Oliver Cowdery were translating the Book of Mormon, they read about baptism. The scriptures said that everyone must be baptized to receive eternal life. But Joseph and Oliver hadn't been baptized. So they went into the woods and knelt to pray. In their prayer, they asked Heavenly Father what they should do.

While Joseph and Oliver were praying, a man came down from heaven in a cloud of light. He was John the Baptist—the same person who had baptized Jesus Christ. John laid his hands on Joseph's and Oliver's heads and gave them the Aaronic Priesthood. Then, he told Joseph and Oliver to go to the river and baptize each other.

Joseph first baptized Oliver, and then Oliver baptized Joseph. When they came up out of the water, both men were filled with the Spirit. They began to prophesy many things about the Church and the gospel.

Why Do We Need to Be Baptized?

There are many reasons we need to be baptized. One reason is to receive a remission of our sins. What does it mean to receive a remission of our sins? Cross out every letter that is in the box five times. Then, starting with the top row of blanks, write all of the leftover letters in order.

H	E	M	A	V	E	K	P	D
N	L	J	Y	F	W	A	T	Z
M	P	H	E	J	R	H	W	J
A	S	M	K	J	Z	F	O	P
R	G	Z	I	V	W	E	N	D
M	Z	K	M	J	Y	O	W	W
U	K	P	D	D	Z	P	D	K

__ __ __ __ __ __ __ __ __

__ __ __ __ __ __

__ __ __ __ __ __ __ __ __

___ ___ ___.

A Commandment Jesus Gave to His Disciples

While Jesus was on the earth, He commanded His disciples to go to all nations and do something. To find out what He told them to do, finish the scripture below. Fill in each blank with the letter from the top that has the same number.

A=1 B=2 C=3 E=4 F=5 G=6 H=7 I=8 L=9 N=10
O=11 P=12 R=13 S=14 T=15 Y=16 Z=17

"GO ___ ___ THEREFORE, AND
    16 4

___ ___ ___ ___ ___ ALL NATIONS,
15 4 1 3 7

___ ___ ___ ___ ___ ___ ___ ___ ___ THEM
2 1 12 15 8 17 8 10 6

IN THE NAME OF THE ___ ___ ___ ___ ___ ___,
  5 1 15 7 4 13

AND OF THE ___ ___ ___, AND OF THE
  14 11 10

___ ___ ___ ___ ___ ___ ___ ___ ___:"
7 11 9 16   6 7 11 14 15

—MATTHEW 28:19

Baptism Is Symbolic

Baptism is symbolic. What does "symbolic" mean? Fill in the blanks with the letter that has the same fruit next to it to find out.

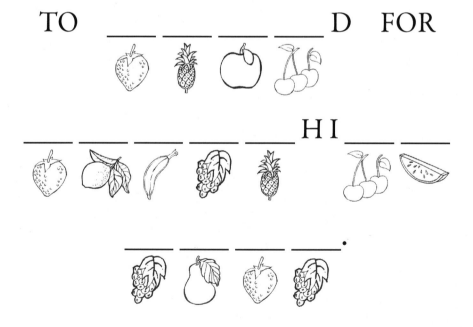

What Does Baptism Symbolize?

Baptism is symbolic of two very important events. This means it *symbolizes* the events. To find out what they are, first fill in the blanks with the letter that has the same object next to it. Then cross out all of the A's in the second word.

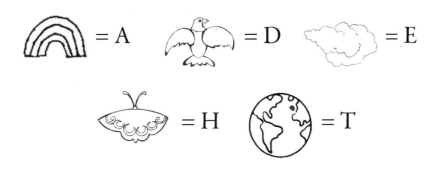

_____ _____ _____ _____ _____

AND

RAESAUARAREACTIAON

_____ _____ _____ _____ _____ _____ _____ _____ _____ _____ _____

Forgiveness of Sins

When we are baptized, our sins are forgiven. How did Jesus make this possible? To find the answer, solve the math problems under each blank. Then write the letter that has the same number as the answer to each math problem in the blanks.

A=7 E=2 G=10 H=8 M=0

N=1 O=6 R=3 T=4 U=9

___ ___ ___ ___ ___ ___ ___   ___ ___ ___
2+2= 5+3= 4–1= 4+2= 7+2= 6+4= 9–1=   6–2= 4+4= 4–2=

___ ___ ___ ___ ___ ___ ___ ___ ___
4+3= 7–3= 3+3= 2–1= 7–5= 9–9= 1+1= 8–7= 8–4=

18

The Atonement of Jesus Christ

Through His Atonement, Jesus Christ paid the price for our sins. He willingly suffered and died so we can be forgiven and resurrected. Color this picture of Jesus in the Garden of Gethsemane.

Becoming a Member of the Church

Another reason we are baptized is to become a member of The Church of Jesus Christ of Latter-day Saints, which is the Lord's true Church. Make your way to the meetinghouse through the maze.

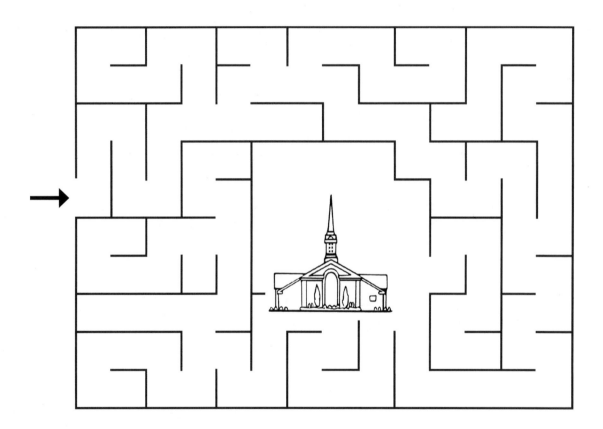

Things We Do as Church Members

Read the list below of some things we do as members of The Church of Jesus Christ of Latter-day Saints. Then find the words in the word search by looking backward, forward, up, and down. Remember to cross out each word as you find it. HINT: Look for each word separately—*pay, tithing, be, missionaries,* etc.

PAY TITHING
BE MISSIONARIES
HELP OUR NEIGHBORS

PARTAKE OF THE SACRAMENT
SERVE IN A CHURCH CALLING
ATTEND CHURCH MEETINGS

```
M I S S I O N A R I E S
T P A Y H C S I O P C B
N H A M E V R E S A H U
E A K T L P O A W R U O
M D E I P S B T A T R C
A C H U R C H T L A C O
R A S I J D G E S K H R
C L T I T H I N G E A S
A L D E H E E D A B O U
S I D N E L N S E C T L
F N E R B P D I N I H X
S G N I T E E M O F E W
```

Our Confirmation

After we are baptized, hands are laid on our head and we are confirmed a member of the Church. As part of this ordinance, we receive a very special gift. To find out what it is, write the names of each picture in the spaces below it. Then read the squares that have a dark line around them to find the answer.

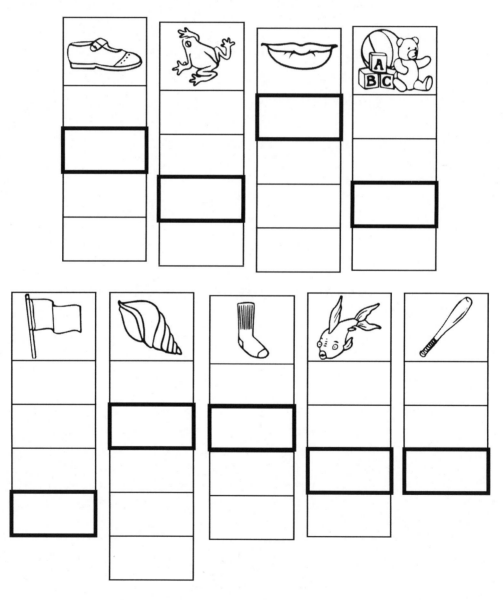

We Receive Something Special

In Moses 6:52, we learn what we need to do to receive a wonderful blessing from Heavenly Father. To see what this verse of scripture says, write the letters in all the blanks that have the same shape.

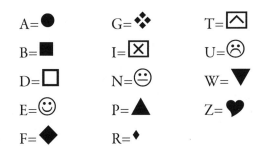

THE LORD SAID, "IF THOU WILT __ __ __ __

UNTO ME, AND . . . ___ ___ ___ ___ ___ ___ OF ALL THY

TRANSGRESSIONS (SINS), AND BE

___ ___ ___ ___ ___ ___ ___ ___, EVEN IN ___ ___ ___ ___ ___,

IN THE NAME OF MINE ONLY BEGOTTEN SON,

. . . YE SHALL RECEIVE THE ___ ___ ___ ___ OF

THE HOLY GHOST."

—MOSES 6:52

Who Is the Holy Ghost?

The Holy Ghost is the third member of the Godhead. To discover one of His main roles, spell the name of each picture, then add or subtract the letters as directed. Write the leftover letters in the blanks. HINT: The first picture is a spear.

– EAR + IRIT =

___ ___ ___ ___ ___ ___

TH + 🐱 – C =

___ ___ ___ ___

GUI + 🗄 – K +

___ ___ ___ ___ ___ ___

🚌 – B =

___ ___.

The Gift of the Holy Ghost

The Holy Ghost helps us in many ways. To find out one thing He helps us to do, go through the maze. The first time a letter crosses your path, write that letter in the first blank at the bottom of the page. The second time a letter crosses your path, write it in the second blank. Continue until you have filled in all of the blanks. HINT: There is only one correct path through the maze.

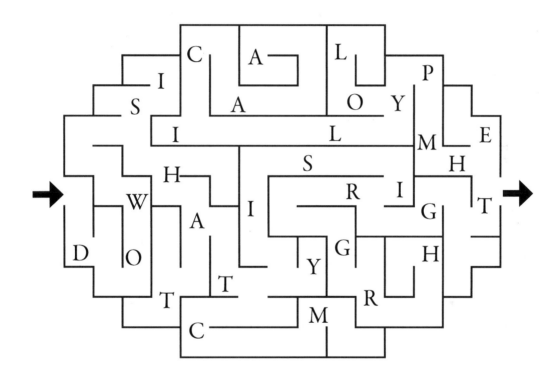

THE HOLY GHOST HELPS US TO

___ ___ ___ ___ ___ ___ ___ ___

___ ___ ___ ___ ___.

The Holy Ghost Helps Us to Be Kind

The Holy Ghost helps us to be kind to others. Write or draw a picture of something that you can do to show kindness to the people around you.

I can show kindness by . . .

The Holy Ghost Testifies

The Holy Ghost always testifies of something. To learn what it is, color the spaces that have a dot.

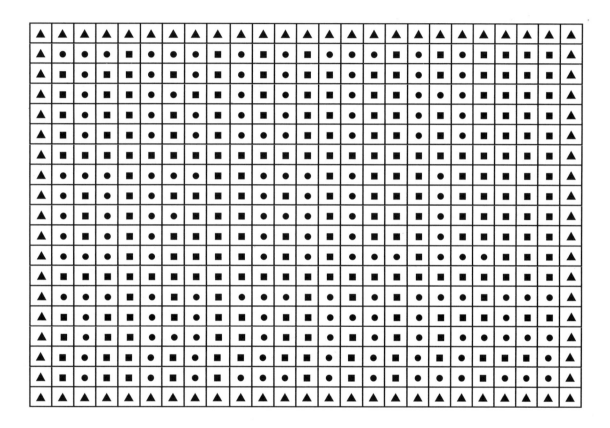

The Holy Ghost Guides Us

If we will listen to His promptings, the Holy Ghost will guide us in what we should do. To see one way He often guides us, cross out every box that has a happy face in it, then write the leftover letters in the blanks.

K ☺	S	T	A ☺	I	L

L	B ☺	S	M	E ☺	A

E ☺	H ☺	L	L	V	G ☺

O	I	G ☺	C	E	A ☺

___ ___ ___ ___ ___   ___ ___ ___ ___ ___

___ ___ ___ ___ ___

Another Way the Holy Ghost Helps Us

To find another way the Holy Ghost helps us, color each box that has an L, O, V, or E.

THE HOLY GHOST . . .

S	C	D	C	H	P	S	A	D	T	S	H	P	H	A	C	J	P	S	A	C	P	P	C	A	S	C	D	J	P	C	S	D
L	L	O	J	V	L	O	S	L	H	C	K	O	H	L	O	V	C	L	O	V	A	L	O	V	A	L	O	V	P	E	L	O
V	P	J	D	O	C	E	S	O	E	S	V	L	A	E	H	D	S	O	P	E	J	O	P	E	D	S	E	J	P	O	D	C
E	A	C	S	V	D	O	P	V	B	V	B	E	D	L	L	C	J	V	S	O	A	V	O	E	C	D	O	J	A	V	E	L
E	S	D	C	O	H	O	J	E	G	A	Z	O	C	O	D	S	A	L	J	L	C	E	L	D	S	A	L	J	C	P	D	O
O	L	E	P	L	V	E	S	E	R	A	Q	L	C	E	P	A	C	E	O	V	D	L	P	V	C	S	E	A	D	L	E	V
P	S	A	D	C	P	S	A	D	I	C	S	J	S	P	A	C	D	S	J	D	S	P	C	S	D	P	A	C	J	D	S	P

. . . US.

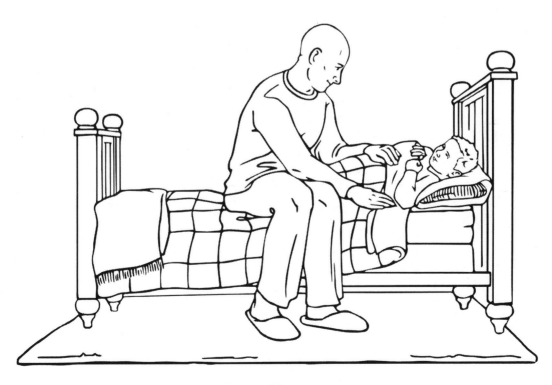

The Holy Ghost Shows Us What to Do

Read the scripture below. Then find all of the underlined words in the word search by looking backward, forward, up, and down. Remember to cross off each word as you find it.

"FOR BEHOLD, AGAIN I SAY UNTO YOU THAT IF YE WILL ENTER

IN BY THE WAY, AND RECEIVE THE HOLY GHOST, IT WILL

SHOW UNTO YOU ALL THINGS WHAT YE SHOULD DO."

—2 NEPHI 32:5

S	E	V	I	E	C	E	R	H
L	O	W	H	A	T	M	E	O
D	C	B	T	D	E	A	K	L
C	R	E	I	L	O	G	U	Y
W	T	H	E	U	S	A	Y	G
B	R	O	F	O	A	I	E	H
M	A	L	P	H	U	N	T	O
A	N	D	F	S	O	D	L	S
J	Y	P	W	A	Y	D	P	T

Why Do We Need to Be Baptized?

When we are baptized, we are showing something very important to our Heavenly Father. To find out what this is, cross out every box with a heart in it. Then write the leftover letters in the blanks.

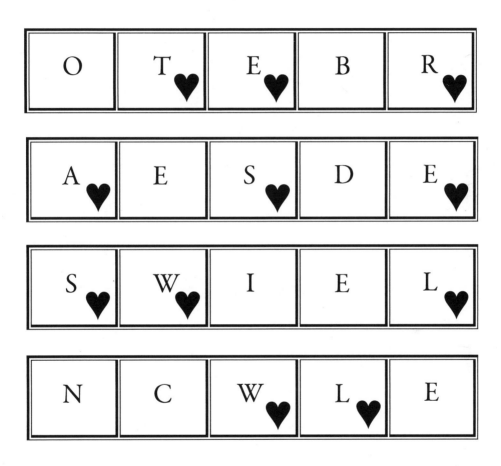

____ ____ ____ ____ ____ ____ ____ ____ ____

Being Obedient to Heavenly Father

What does it mean to be obedient to Heavenly Father? Finish the pattern in each row. Then write the letter in the blanks with the same number.

DDT YYA DDT YY___

1

JJK JJD JJK JJ___

2

HUE HUE HU___

3

GFRH GFRH GFR___

4

HIJKL HIJKL HIJK___

5

MMM OOO MMM OO___

6

B BU BUS B BU BU___

7

PQ PQR PQRS PQRS___

8

SLDU SLDU SLD___

9

TT UU VV W___

10

___ ___ ___ ___ ___ ___ ___ ___ ___ ___

10 3   2 6   10 4 1 8   4 3

___ ___ ___ ___ ___ ___ ___ ___ ___ ___ ___ .

8 3 5 5 7   9 7   8 6   2 6

Jesus Was Obedient to Heavenly Father

Even though Jesus never committed any sins, He was baptized to be obedient to Heavenly Father. Read the scripture verses below, then color the picture of Jesus being baptized by John the Baptist.

"But he that sent me to baptize with water, the same said unto me, Upon whom thou shalt see the Spirit descending, and remaining on him, the same is he which baptizeth with the Holy Ghost.

"And I saw, and bare record that this is the Son of God."

—John 1:33–34

To Live in a Special Place

We also need to be baptized so we can live in a special place one day. To find the name of that place, cross out all the P's, Z's, B's, and U's. Then write the leftover letters in order in the blanks, starting with the top row.

P Z B U Z B P U B Z

U P U C E L Z B U P

Z E P S Z T I U B Z

Z B A L K I Z U P B

B N G P D B O U Z P

U Z U M U Z P U B Z

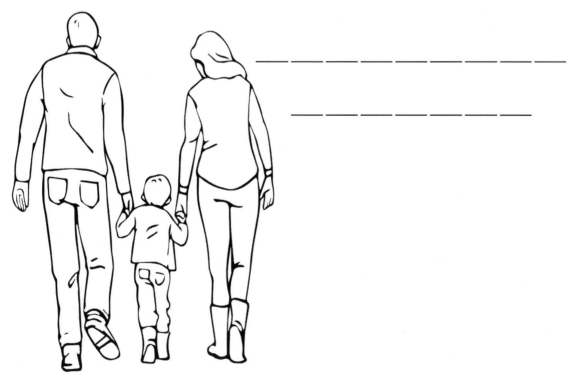

__ __ __ __ __ __ __ __ __ __

__ __ __ __ __ __ __

A Baptism Story: Alma at the Waters of Mormon

When the prophet Abinadi taught the gospel of Jesus Christ to wicked King Noah and his priests, only one person believed Abinadi. That person's name was Alma. He tried to stand up for Abinadi so he would not be hurt. But King Noah got angry at Alma too. He sent servants to kill Alma, but Alma hid. He wrote down all the words of Abinadi so they would not be lost.

Alma secretly began to teach people the words of Abinadi. The believers gathered in the wilderness in a place called Mormon. It had trees where they could hide, and a fountain of pure water called the waters of Mormon.

One day when Alma was teaching the people, he said, "Behold, here are the waters of Mormon . . . and now, as ye are desirous to come into the fold of God, and to be called his people, . . . what have ye against being baptized in the name of the Lord?" (Mosiah 18:8, 10).

The people were excited. They clapped their hands and told Alma that this was what they wanted most of all. So he began to baptize them. First he took a man named Helam down into the waters of Mormon. Helam was baptized just like we are today—by immersion.

Alma baptized 204 people that day. Everyone who was baptized became a member of the Church of Christ.

The Way We Are Baptized

The Lord told us how we should be baptized. Write the letter from each shape in the matching blank below to find out how baptism is to be done.

E=↑   I=⇨   M=⊙   Y=□
N=❖   O=⦚   R=⊘   S=▷

We are baptized b __
□

__ __ __ __ __ __ __ __ __ .
⇨   ⊙   ⊙   ↑   ⊘   ▷   ⇨   ⦚   ❖

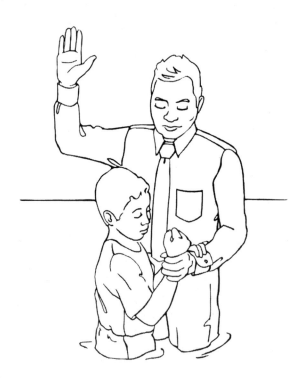

The Way We Are Baptized

What does it mean to be baptized by immersion? Fill in the blanks with the vowels that are missing from each word. Cross off each vowel as you use it.

A E E E E I O U U

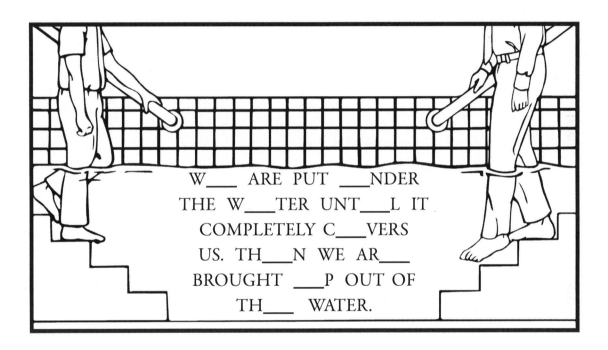

W___ ARE PUT ___NDER THE W___TER UNT___L IT COMPLETELY C___VERS US. TH___N WE AR___ BROUGHT ___P OUT OF TH___ WATER.

Instructions for Baptism

In Doctrine and Covenants 20:73–74, Jesus Christ tells Joseph Smith how baptism should be done. Read those scripture verses below. Then find all of the underlined words in the word search by looking forward, backward, up, and down. Remember to cross off each word as you find it.

"The <u>person</u> who is <u>called</u> of God and has <u>authority</u>
from <u>Jesus Christ</u> to <u>baptize</u>, shall go down into the <u>water</u>
with the person who has presented himself or herself for <u>baptism</u>,
and shall say, calling him or her by name: Having been
commissioned of Jesus Christ, I baptize you in the name of
the <u>Father</u>, and of the <u>Son</u>, and of the <u>Holy Ghost</u>. Amen.
"Then shall he <u>immerse</u> him or her in the water,
and come forth again out of the water."

H	F	A	T	H	E	R	T	S	Z
H	U	P	I	Y	N	E	S	L	D
O	A	U	T	H	O	R	I	T	Y
L	I	S	I	P	S	O	R	C	N
Y	F	B	M	O	R	A	H	S	M
G	C	A	M	L	E	L	C	O	S
H	W	P	E	A	P	I	A	N	I
O	A	T	R	M	R	N	L	S	T
S	T	I	S	V	T	I	L	B	P
T	E	Z	E	Z	J	I	E	E	A
W	R	E	D	I	O	O	D	M	B

We Make Sacred Promises

When we are baptized, we make sacred promises with Heavenly Father. These sacred promises are called the _____ of baptism. To find the word that goes in the blank, write the first letter of the name of each picture in the boxes underneath them.

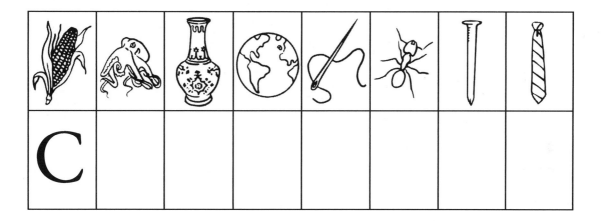

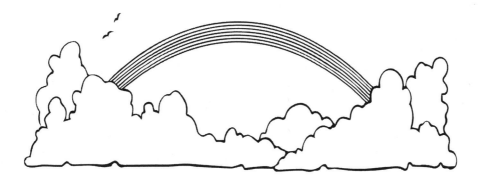

What Is a Covenant?

To find out what a covenant is, match each picture with its shadow and write the letter from that box in order in the blanks.

_____ _____ _____ _____ _____ _____

What Do We Become at Our Baptism?

We become something when we are baptized. To find out what that is, make your way through the maze. Then write each letter that crosses your path in order in the blanks.

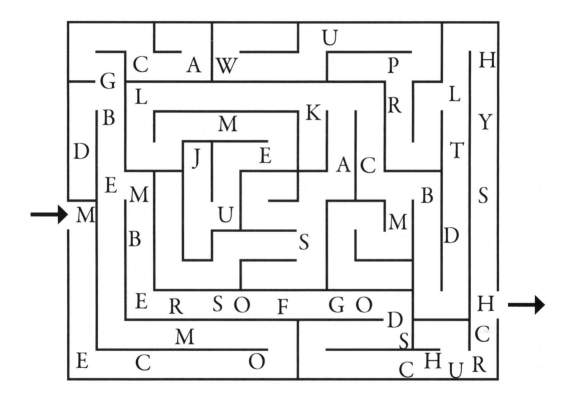

When we are baptized, we become __ __ __ __ __ __ __

__ __ __ __ __ ' __ __ __ __ __ __ __ __.

A Promise We Make at Baptism

When we are baptized, we make many promises to the Lord. To find out one thing we promise Him we will do, follow the instructions below. Once you have added and subtracted the letters, write the leftover letters in the blanks.

TALL – LL + KE   UNTO – NTO + PON

___ ___ ___ ___ ___   ___ ___ ___ ___ ___

BUS – B   H + ISN'T – N'T

___ ___ ___   ___ ___ ___

NAP – P + ME

___ ___ ___ ___

A Promise We Make at Baptism

To discover something we promise to be after we are baptized, cross out each box that has a CTR shield in it. Write the rest of the letters in the blanks.

J	W	I	T	O	N	E
S	D	F	S	F	P	O
R	C	H	R	E	F	I
S	T	S	A	N	D	H
I	G	S	C	H	U	I
R	T	Y	H	C	H	P

A __ __ __ __ __ __ __   __ __ __   __ __ __ __ __ __

__ __ __   __ __ __   __ __ __ __ __ __

A Promise We Make at Baptism

Some of the words below are scrambled. To unscramble them, cross out all of the Z's and L's. Write the leftover letters in the blanks. Then you will know another thing we promise to do when we are baptized.

WE COVENANT TO:

SLLEZLRLZZVLZLE   LZEALLZCH

— — — — —   — — — —

OZTZHLLEZR   ALZND   BEZZLLZAR

— — — — —   — — —   — — — —

OZZLLLNLE   ZZLALNOTLLZLHERZS

— — —   — — — — — — — —

ZLBZULRDELLZZNZS

— — — — — —

A Promise We Make at Baptism

To find out another thing we promise to do when we are baptized, trace over the dots. When you finish, color the picture.

A Promise We Make at Baptism

To see another thing we promise Heavenly Father when we are baptized, cross out all the CAPITAL letters in each line. Write the leftover letters on the lines below.

We covenant to . . .

TsLEeAPMrYUvSe   GhMim

_____   _____

JaKWMnEAd   BkeTWHASep

_____   _____

hEWViBHs   comEDXmLanSOdmenYts

_____   _____ .

A Promise from Heavenly Father

As we are baptized and make promises with Heavenly Father, He also makes promises to us. To discover one of His promises to us, write the letters for each shape in the blanks with the matching shape.

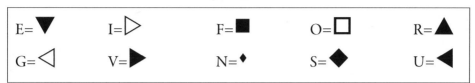

IF WE KEEP OUR COVENANTS, HEAVENLY FATHER WILL . . .

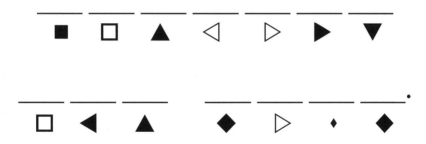

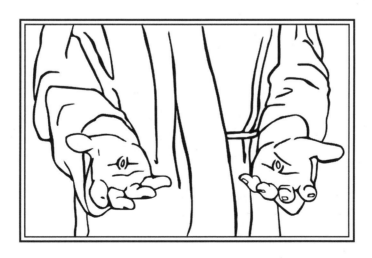

A Promise from Heavenly Father

To find another one of Heavenly Father's promises to us if we keep our baptismal covenants, follow the arrows from picture to picture. As you come to a picture, write its first letter in the blanks. Be sure to write the letters in order.

START

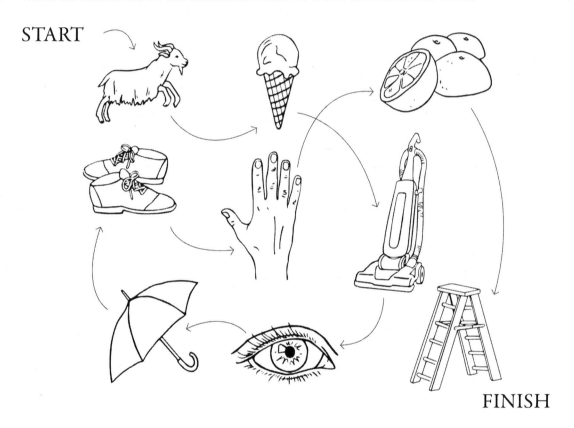

FINISH

HEAVENLY FATHER PROMISES TO

____ ____ ____ ____   ____ ____ THE GUIDANCE

OF THE ____ ____ ____ Y   GHOST.

A Promise from Heavenly Father

Each of the missing letters has an arrow pointing to the blank where the letter belongs. To reveal something Heavenly Father promises us if we keep our covenants, follow the arrows and write each letter in its correct space.

G ___ ___ E   ___ ___

E ___ E ___ N ___ ___ ___

___ I F ___

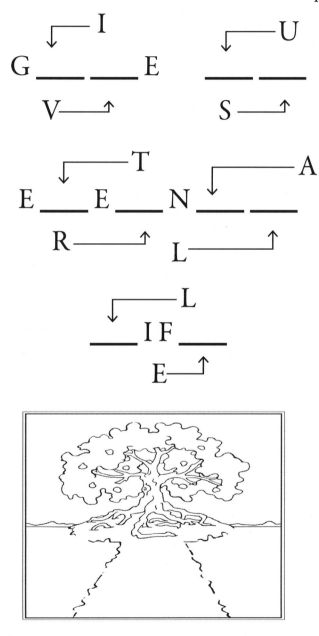

A Promise from Heavenly Father

Cross out all of the lowercase letters below. Then write the leftover letters in order in the blanks. Now you know another one of Heavenly Father's promises to us if we keep the promises we make to Him at baptism.

HEAVENLY FATHER PROMISES THAT WE WILL . . .

COnbMarsE   FweaORvxTosH

_____   _____

uIsnmeN   TmpHEe   kmspFIearRppSnT

____   ____   _____

dfrRElsSmwiUrclsRRioECghTIObvN

_____ .

What Does "Resurrection" Mean?

In the first row below, cross out the word "JESUS." Then write the leftover letters in the blanks. In the second row, cross out the word "LOVES" and write the leftover letters in the blanks. Do this for each row to find out what "resurrection" means.

RESURRECTION MEANS TO:

1. JESUS . . . JBRIESUSNG   ___ ___ ___ ___ ___

2. LOVES . . . LBAOVECKS   ___ ___ ___ ___

3. US . . . TOUGETHSER   ___ ___ ___ ___ ___ ___ ___

4. AND . . . TANHDE   ___ ___ ___

5. WILLINGLY . . . WILLBOIDNGLYY   ___ ___ ___ ___

6. GAVE . . . GWITAVEH   ___ ___ ___ ___

7. HIS . . . THHEIS   ___ ___ ___

8. LIFE . . . SPLIIRFEIT   ___ ___ ___ ___ ___

9. FOR . . . FFOORR   ___ ___ ___

10. US . . . EUTERNISTY   ___ ___ ___ ___ ___ ___ ___

The Morning of the First Resurrection

Everyone born on the earth will be resurrected. But only those who have kept God's commandments and endured to the end will come forth in the morning of the first resurrection. What does it mean to come forth in the morning of the first resurrection? To find out, start at #1 and write the CAPITAL letters in the blanks with the same number.

1. YmOnnwU
2. WmnopILsL
3. vbqrLIVaeE
4. WiiITHsa
5. HEwAmVjENLfgy
6. ssFteaaATHsErrR
7. ANqweD
8. JEsmpSmnUzS
9. FwpzceOREsfVEmnR

1. ___ ___ ___   2. ___ ___ ___ ___

3. ___ ___ ___ ___   4. ___ ___ ___ ___

5. ___ ___ ___ ___ ___ ___ ___

6. ___ ___ ___ ___ ___ ___

7. ___ ___ ___   8. ___ ___ ___ ___ ___

9. ___ ___ ___ ___ ___ ___ ___ .

Baptism Stories: Three Apostles

President Wilford Woodruff: A young man named Wilford Woodruff was baptized in a river in the middle of winter. He had first heard of the gospel at a meeting in a schoolhouse. After the meeting, he invited the missionaries to his home. He was baptized the next day. Wilford Woodruff became a great missionary and baptized 2,000 people. At age 32, he was ordained a member of the Quorum of the Twelve Apostles. Fifty years later, he became the President of the Church.

President Dieter F. Uchtdorf: Did you know that Dieter F. Uchtdorf was baptized in a swimming pool? His family lived in Zwickau, Germany, after World War II. They met for church in a cold, crowded back room where there was often no electricity. But Dieter and his family knew the Church was true. Many years later he became a member of the Quorum of the Twelve Apostles, and he is now a counselor in the First Presidency.

Elder David B. Haight: One day, David B. Haight was playing in an irrigation canal with his friends and saw his father, the bishop, walking out of the ward meetinghouse with his two counselors. He said, "David, come on over here—we're going to baptize you." David's father baptized him, and then he and his counselors confirmed him on the chair they had brought. David later became a member of the Quorum of the Twelve Apostles.

With Proper Authority

Someone with the proper priesthood authority will baptize us. It could be our dad, uncle, grandfather, bishop, or another Church member who holds the Melchizedek Priesthood. In each sentence, cross out every letter that appears four times. Then write the leftover letters in order on the line underneath each one.

NPRLNILESNTLHOLOND

_____

PGFOFGWGFEGRF

_____

Your Baptism

Draw a picture of the priesthood holder who is going to baptize you.

Eight Is Great!

When you turn eight years old, you become accountable for what you do. What does "accountable" mean? To find out, cross out all the names of fruit and all the names of bugs. Then read what is left over.

Ladybug	Tomato	Being	Able	Cherry
Strawberry	Banana	To	Spider	Fly
Understand	Orange	Dragonfly	Right	Worm
From	Blueberry	Beetle	Lemon	Apple
Mosquito	Raspberry	Wrong	Peach	Pear

The Color We Wear at Our Baptism

The color of the clothing we wear for our baptism is very important. To find out what it is, color in all of the boxes with an X. After you know the color you will wear at your baptism, get some colored pencils and color the picture below.

Y	Y	Y	Y	Y	Y	Y	Y	Y	Y	Y	Y	Y	Y	Y	Y	Y	Y	Y	Y	Y	Y	Y	Y	Y	Y	Y	Y	Y	Y	Y	Y
Y	X	Y	Y	Y	X	Y	X	Y	Y	X	Y	X	X	X	X	X	Y	X	X	X	X	Y	X	X	X	X	X	Y	Y	Y	Y
Y	X	Y	Y	Y	X	Y	X	Y	Y	X	Y	Y	Y	X	Y	Y	Y	X	Y	Y	Y	X	Y	Y	Y	Y	Y	Y	Y	Y	Y
Y	X	Y	X	Y	X	Y	X	X	X	X	Y	Y	Y	X	Y	Y	Y	Y	Y	X	Y	Y	Y	X	X	X	X	Y	Y	Y	Y
Y	X	X	Y	X	X	Y	X	Y	Y	X	Y	Y	Y	X	Y	Y	Y	Y	Y	X	Y	Y	Y	X	Y	Y	Y	Y	Y	Y	Y
Y	X	Y	Y	Y	X	Y	X	Y	Y	X	Y	X	X	X	X	X	Y	Y	Y	X	Y	Y	Y	X	X	X	X	X	Y	Y	Y
Y	Y	Y	Y	Y	Y	Y	Y	Y	Y	Y	Y	Y	Y	Y	Y	Y	Y	Y	Y	Y	Y	Y	Y	Y	Y	Y	Y	Y	Y	Y	Y

57

White Is Symbolic

The color white is a symbol of purity. What does "purity" mean? In each word below, cross out all of the J's and T's. Then write the leftover letters in the spaces.

JJTJFJRJETTEJTJT

—— —— —— —— ——

JJTJJFJJROJTTJTJMJTT

—— —— —— —— ——

SJTTJTIJTJJNTTJ

—— —— —— ——

Preparing for Baptism

Before we get baptized we should prepare ourselves. What does "prepare" mean? To find out, cross out all of the double letters in each line. Then write the leftover letters in the blanks.

YYTUUPPLLMMONN

___ ___

LLSSEEGPPEZZAAT

___ ___ ___

GGRMMEAPPRRDCCYII

___ ___ ___ ___ ___

Preparing for Baptism

To learn one thing we should do often as part of preparing to be baptized, write the first letter of each picture in the blank under it. Then read the word, starting with the letter under the peas.

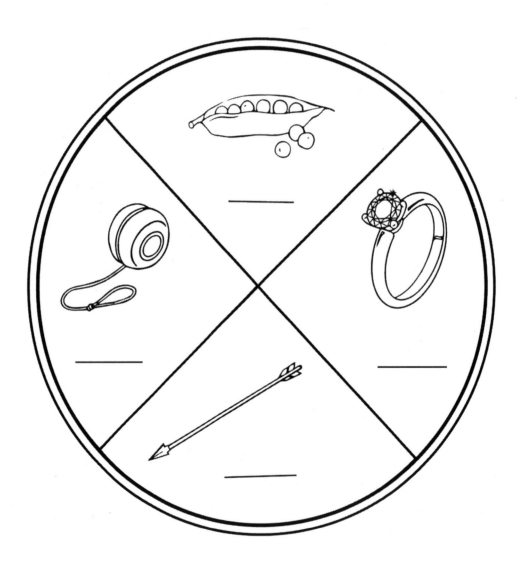

Praying to Heavenly Father

Being able to pray to Heavenly Father is a great blessing. Go through the letter maze. Cross out every A, V, F, and G. Write the leftover letters in the blanks below to discover one thing we can do when we pray.

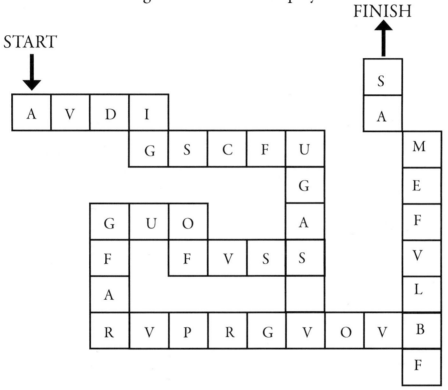

START

FINISH

WHEN WE PRAY, WE CAN . . .

—— —— —— —— —— —— ——   —— —— ——

—— —— —— —— —— —— —— ——.

An Important Part of Prayer

Prayer also helps us express something to our Heavenly Father. To find out what it is, write the name of each picture in the blanks with the same number, then read the word spelled out in the darker boxes.

Whom Does Prayer Keep Us Close To?

Prayer keeps us close to someone. Read each sentence. If the sentence is true, color the letter in the TRUE row. If it is not true, color the letter in the FALSE row. Starting with #1, copy the colored letters onto the blanks below. Beginning again from #1, go back and copy the uncolored letters onto the rest of the blanks.

	TRUE	FALSE
1. We should fold our arms when we pray.	H	Y
2. We should pray about the same things every night.	F	E
3. We should pray when the TV is on.	A	A
4. We should only pray when we feel like it.	T	V
5. We should pray for others.	E	H
6. We should bow our heads and close our eyes when we pray.	N	E
7. We should thank Heavenly Father every time we pray.	L	R

PRAYER HELPS KEEP US CLOSE TO OUR

___ ___ ___ ___ ___ ___ ___ ___

___ ___ ___ ___ ___ ___.

Being Sincere in Our Prayers

When we pray, it is important that we are sincere. What does "sincere" mean? To find out, trace the path to each star to find the words for each line. Write the words in the lines with the same number.

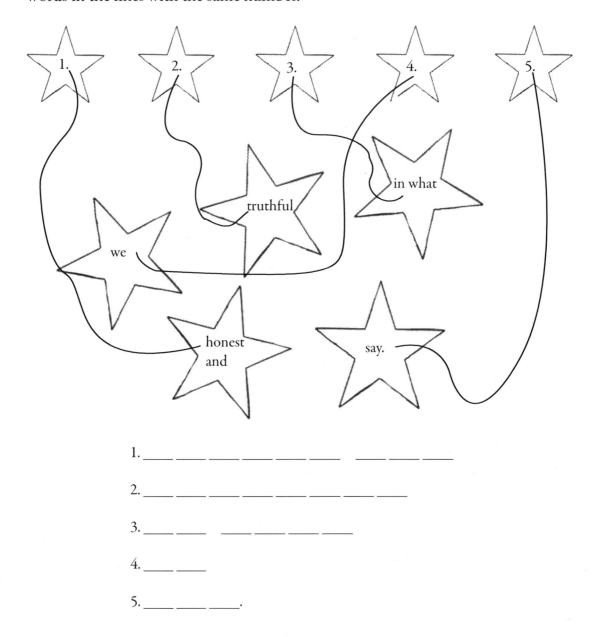

1. ___ ___ ___ ___ ___ ___ ___ ___ ___

2. ___ ___ ___ ___ ___ ___ ___

3. ___ ___ ___ ___ ___ ___

4. ___ ___

5. ___ ___ ___.

What We Do on Sunday

We can also prepare for our baptism by doing something every Sunday. To find out what it is, start with the first row and cross out the letters in the parentheses, then write the leftover letters in the blanks. When you have done this for each row, you will know what you need to do every week on the Sabbath.

(EIGHT) EAITTEGHNTD

— — — — — — —

(IS) CHIURSCH

— — — — — —

(GREAT) MEGREEATTINGS

— — — — — — — —

Attending Church Meetings

Why is it important to attend Church meetings? To find out one reason, go through the maze and write the first letter of each picture in the blanks.

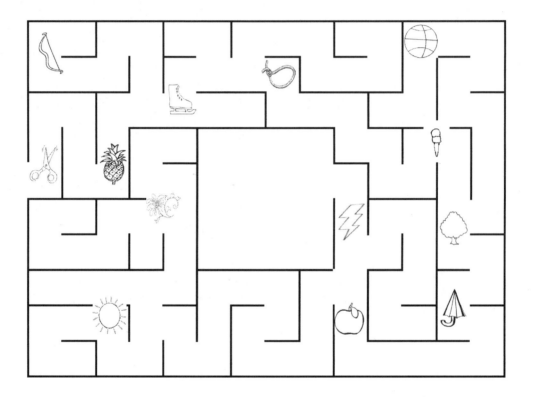

WE ATTEND CHURCH MEETINGS TO GAIN

____ ____ ____ ____ ____ ____ ____ ____ ____ STRENGTH.

One Reason We Attend Church Meetings

Solve each of the math problems below. Then cross out each box where the answer is 4. Read the leftover letters to find another reason why attending our Church meetings is important.

IT MAKES OUR...

T $4 + 2 =$ ___	Y $2 + 2 =$ ___	E $3 + 5 =$ ___	R $6 - 2 =$ ___	S $6 - 3 =$ ___	T $7 + 3 =$ ___
I $3 + 2 =$ ___	G $3 + 1 =$ ___	M $5 + 5 =$ ___	O $1 + 9 =$ ___	U $8 - 4 =$ ___	N $3 + 3 =$ ___
Y $9 - 5 =$ ___	I $5 + 2 =$ ___	E $2 + 6 =$ ___	R $7 - 3 =$ ___	S $7 + 4 =$ ___	O $4 + 0 =$ ___

___ ___ ___ ___ ___ ___ ___ ___ ___ ___ STRONGER.

What We Do at Church

What should we do when we are at church? To find out, unscramble the words in the boxes by writing all of the parts of words in the empty boxes that have the same number.

WHEN WE ARE AT CHURCH WE SHOULD . . .

2. REV	7. PON	6. NG	4. NT
5. SI	3. ERE	1. BE	8. DER

1.	2.	3.	4.
5.	6.	7.	8.

Another Way We Prepare for Baptism

To find out something we should read and study to help prepare for baptism, write down the word that goes with each clue in the blanks. Then write the letters from the dark boxes in the boxes at the bottom.

1. Something you wear on your feet.

2. You go here every Sunday.

3. You do this in a race.

4. You put this in a drink to make it cold.

5. When the light is red you should do this.

6. If you add 1 + 1, you get this number.

7. This shines in the daytime.

8. This is the color of grass.

9. These are the things on your head that help you hear.

10. These are the things on your face that help you see.

READ AND STUDY THE . . .

Preparing by Reading the Scriptures

To find out one way reading the scriptures helps us, cross out all of the words that are in pictures of pears. Then cross out all of the words that are in pictures of books. Write the leftover words in the blanks with the same numbers.

HELPS US UNDERSTAND WHAT

1._____ FATHER 2._____ US

3._____ 4._____.

Preparing by Reading the Scriptures

Cross off every C, D, G, Z, and A. Write the leftover letters from left to right in the blanks to find out another thing reading the scriptures does for us.

Reading the scriptures helps us . . .

D G Z A F E G A D E

C D G Z L T G D A H

E Z G C A D C Z S P

I Z A R Z G C D I G

A C D G T Z D A G Z

__ __ __ __   __ __ __   __ __ __ __ __ __ __ .

Preparing by Fasting

What does fasting do for us? To find out, choose the word that is the right one for each sentence. Then put the circled letters from the boxes with the right words in order in the blanks in the plate.

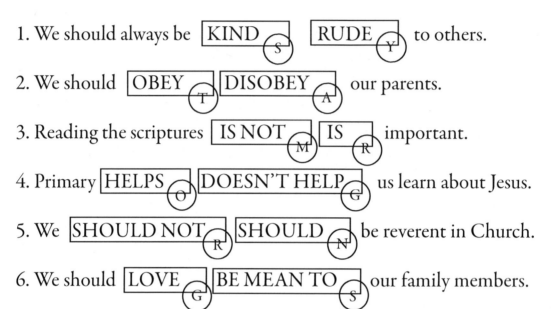

1. We should always be [KIND Ⓢ] [RUDE Ⓨ] to others.

2. We should [OBEY Ⓣ] [DISOBEY Ⓐ] our parents.

3. Reading the scriptures [IS NOT Ⓜ] [IS Ⓡ] important.

4. Primary [HELPS Ⓞ] [DOESN'T HELP Ⓖ] us learn about Jesus.

5. We [SHOULD NOT Ⓡ] [SHOULD Ⓝ] be reverent in Church.

6. We should [LOVE Ⓖ] [BE MEAN TO Ⓢ] our family members.

FASTING MAKES US SPIRITUALLY...

___ ___ ___ ___ ___ ___.
1. 2. 3. 4. 5. 6.

Preparing by Fasting

Fasting is also a way to ask Heavenly Father for something important to us. What might we ask for when we fast? Cross out all of the words that have to do with wintertime. Read the leftover words to find out.

● SNOWMAN

● MITTENS

● SPECIAL HELP

● KNOWLEDGE

● BLESSINGS

● SLEDDING

● COLD

● SNOWFLAKE

Preparing by Fasting

Whom can we fast for? Follow the direction of the arrows through the letter maze. Write each letter at the end of the arrows in the blanks to find out.

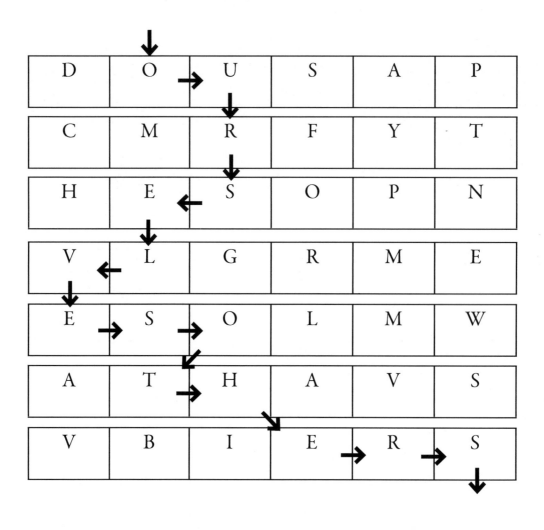

___ ___ ___ ___ ___ ___ ___ ___ ___ ___

AND ___ ___ ___ ___ ___ ___

A Baptism Story: John and Jesus

John the Baptist lived in the wilderness of Jordan. He wore clothing made from camels' hair, and shoes made of leather. For his food, he ate locusts and honey. Many people came from Jerusalem and Judea to listen to John preach. He taught them to repent and that Christ would come. John baptized people who believed.

One day John the Baptist had a special visitor. His name was Jesus. Jesus asked John to baptize him. John was surprised. He didn't think that he was worthy to baptize Jesus, because he knew Jesus was the Son of God. Jesus told John that He needed to be baptized to keep God's commandments.

John baptized Jesus in the Jordan River. When Jesus came up out of the water, the heavens opened, and the Holy Ghost descended upon him like a dove.

At Jesus' baptism, He and John heard Heavenly Father's voice from heaven, saying, "This is my beloved Son, in whom I am well pleased." Heavenly Father will be happy when YOU are baptized, too.

Renewing Our Baptismal Covenants

Each Sunday we renew our baptismal covenants. To learn how we do this, find the hidden letter on each flower and write it in the blanks with the same number.

____ ____ RT ____ ____ ____ OF THE
 6   2   2   1   5

S ____ ____ R ____ M ____ ____ T
   2   4   2   5   3

Partaking of the Sacrament

What happens when we partake of the sacrament? To find out, match each picture with its shadow, then write the words from the picture in the blank underneath each matching shadow.

Partaking of the Sacrament

Read what it means to renew our covenants. Then find all of the words in the word search. HINT: Cross off each word as you find it.

When we renew our covenants, we promise Heavenly Father again that we will keep them.

```
E  V  C  E  W  H  O  N  E  A  S
S  T  N  A  N  E  V  O  C  O  M
I  O  U  R  F  A  W  E  K  P  E
M  W  E  E  C  V  E  G  E  O  H
O  H  B  A  I  E  P  E  L  L  T
R  E  N  E  W  N  L  S  P  M  N
P  W  I  L  L  L  B  G  Y  P  I
T  H  A  T  O  Y  W  A  R  L  A
N  H  Y  O  W  F  W  A  L  N  G
B  C  E  T  R  A  L  O  P  U  A
M  K  T  F  K  T  P  D  B  C  M
W  H  E  N  J  H  R  C  D  L  P
X  Z  F  R  U  E  L  P  O  U  R
U  B  U  O  R  R  J  M  C  D  U
```

Partaking of the Sacrament

Partaking of the sacrament helps us remember something. Under each word below are directions that tell you to do something with that word. After you have followed the directions under each word, write the leftover letters in the blanks. Then you will know what taking the sacrament helps us remember.

1. ETHEEEE
Cross out 4 E's.

2. URAESAMSPOHNWS
Starting at U, cross out every other letter.

3. TWRHUEY
Cross our the word "TRUE."

4. EAW
Cross out the A.
Then put the W before the E.

5. WEEERRRE
Cross out 3 E's and 2 R's.

6. BLOVAPTEIZED
Cross out the word "LOVE."

IT HELPS US REMEMBER . . .

1. ___ ___ ___   2. ___ ___ ___ ___ ___ ___ ___

3. ___ ___ ___   4. ___ ___   5. ___ ___ ___ ___

6. ___ ___ ___ ___ ___ ___ ___ ___.

The Bread Helps Us Remember

The bread and water we partake of during the sacrament are symbolic. They help us remember something important. What does the bread help us remember? To find out, write the letters in the blanks with the same number.

IT HELPS US REMEMBER THE

___ O ___ ___ OF
9   6   2

___ ___ ___ ___ ___   ___ ___ RI ___ T.
7   5   1   4   1   3   8   1

The Water Helps Us Remember

What does partaking of the water during the sacrament help us remember about the Atonement of Jesus Christ? To find out, read the scripture verse below. Then write the underlined letters in the blanks.

For, be<u>h</u>old, <u>I</u> <u>s</u>ay un<u>to</u> you, that it mattereth n<u>o</u>t what ye shall eat or what ye shall <u>d</u>rink when ye partake of <u>t</u>he sacram<u>e</u>nt, if it <u>s</u>o be <u>t</u>hat ye do it with an <u>e</u>ye single to my glory—remembering unto the Father my bo<u>d</u>y which was laid down <u>f</u>or you, and my blood which was shed f<u>o</u>r the remission of you<u>r</u> sins.

THE WATER HELPS US REMEMBER

___ ___ ___ BL ___ ___ ___ THAT ___ ___

___ ___ ___ D ___ ___ ___ US.

We Become Responsible

After we are baptized, we become responsible for our choices. This means that when we break one of God's commandments, we must do something to become clean and pure again. What must we do after we break a commandment? Write the name of each picture in the spaces with the same number. The dark boxes will reveal the answer.

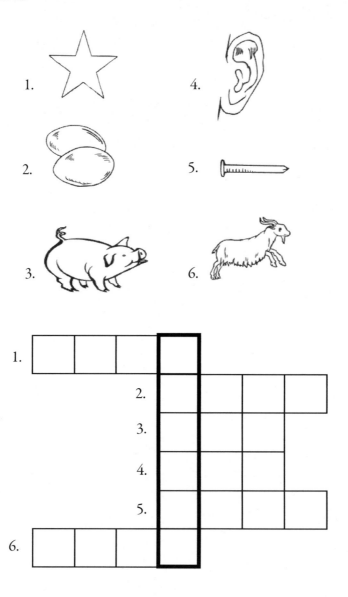

Repentance

It is important to repent after we do something wrong. To learn what it means to repent, read the sentence below, then find all of the words from it in the word search. Make sure you cross out each word as you find it.

Repenting means feeling sorry for what you have done, asking forgiveness, and never committing that sin again.

```
J A R E P E N T I N G
A I B N D E V A H Y N
C S N E V E R H P I I
W E S R O P I W O D L
X A R A G A I N L O E
S G S N A E M F L N E
I N S D E U E O L E F
N I S A S O R R Y U T
T K A R C Y D V P I U
S S E N E V I G R O F
C A T H A T I T R I M
C O M M I T T I N G P
```

Repentance

Because of the sacrifice Jesus made for us, we can repent of our sins and be forgiven. Read the verse of scripture. Then find all of the circled words in the word search. Be sure to look backward, forward, up, and down.

"FOR, BEHOLD, THE LORD YOUR REDEEMER SUFFERED DEATH IN THE FLESH; WHEREFORE HE SUFFERED THE PAIN OF ALL MEN, THAT ALL MEN MIGHT REPENT AND COME UNTO HIM."

—DOCTRINE AND COVENANTS 18:11

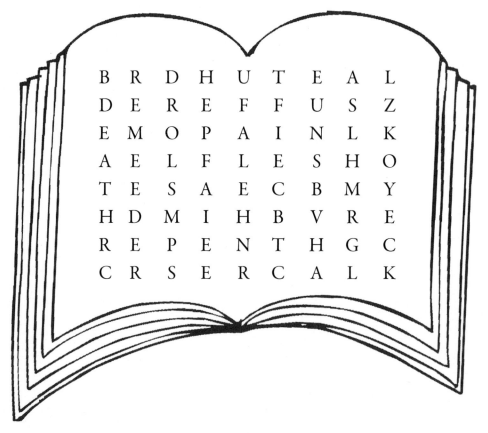

```
B  R  D  H  U  T  E  A  L
D  E  R  E  F  F  U  S  Z
E  M  O  P  A  I  N  L  K
A  E  L  F  L  E  S  H  O
T  E  S  A  E  C  B  M  Y
H  D  M  I  H  B  V  R  E
R  E  P  E  N  T  H  G  C
C  R  S  E  R  C  A  L  K
```

My Baptism Day

Fill in the information about your own special baptism day.

My Full Name: _____

Person Who Baptized Me: _____

Date: _____

Where I Was Baptized: _____

Person Who Confirmed Me: _____

Date: _____

Where I Was Confirmed: _____

People Who Were There: _____

_____

_____

_____

Other Things: _____

_____

_____

_____

_____

_____

_____

_____

My Baptism Day

Draw a picture of what your baptism looked like.

What Did We Learn?

Color this picture of the Savior. Then do the word searches and crossword puzzles that make up the rest of this book. If you need help with the crossword puzzles, go back through the book and look up the answers.

Gospel Principles and Ordinances

ACROSS

1. THIS IS THE FIRST ORDINANCE OF THE GOSPEL.

3. THIS IS THE FIRST PRINCIPLE OF THE GOSPEL.

5. THIS IS THE SECOND PRINCIPLE OF THE GOSPEL.

DOWN

2. THERE ARE _____ AND ORDINANCES OF THE GOSPEL THAT WE MUST LEARN AND OBEY.

4. A PRINCIPLE IS A BELIEF OR A _____.

6. HAVING FAITH MEANS TO HOPE FOR THINGS WHICH ARE NOT SEEN WHICH ARE _____.

Gospel Principles and Ordinances

```
C C H A P E B M E F E L G H U
W R E B Q E C C K G L A X E C
D W M R L A N G F P W V G C
U S A I E A B J A V I D L J O
A Z E M N M J K O T C U N X I
Q F Q I Z C O N R A N U L E S
H M D S S R H N N P I E I N N
Y R S S M E Q Y Y B R A P N S
O F Y V B W T H L A P R Z E L
R Z I Z M M J I J P B T P X R
T E A C H I N G R T B K D C L
Q M C G T T Q C E I U T F M Y
I S V U K V P G C S X H V N B
Q K C Q B U C N H M H T I A F
A G V C N A Y T V Q S B J S T
```

BAPTISM	BELIEF	CEREMONY
FAITH	ORDINANCE	PRINCIPLE
REPENTANCE	RITE	TEACHING

Why We Need to Be Baptized

ACROSS

2. BAPTISM IS SYMBOLIC OF
_____ AND RESURRECTION.

5. WE SHOW OBEDIENCE TO
HEAVENLY _____ WHEN WE ARE
BAPTIZED.

6. JESUS SUFFERED AND _____
FOR US SO THAT WE COULD BE
FORGIVEN.

7. JESUS MADE IT POSSIBLE FOR US
TO BE FORGIVEN OF OUR _____
THROUGH THE ATONEMENT.

DOWN

1. WE SERVE IN CHURCH _____
WHEN WE ARE MEMBERS OF THE
CHURCH.

3. JESUS TOLD HIS APOSTLES
THAT ALL NATIONS SHOULD BE

_____.

4. WE BECOME _____ OF THE
CHURCH OF JESUS CHRIST OF
LATTER-DAY SAINTS AFTER WE ARE
BAPTIZED.

Why We Need to Be Baptized

R E M I S S I O N O F S I N S S
I E F Q H O B C A R D T T D V
L H S V B D N T J E R Y I R K
S O P U P K O A N B P X D E Y
R C H N R N J E S U S H T B O
F E V K E R A X W F X J K M I
T Q H M M O E T P X Q S N E H
C K E T V D E C K H V N U M O
K N X D A I Q Q T V V O X F L
T O C N B F E Z S I A W R V Y
L M F E H Q I P K D O W H T G
I V V T X N O D X W M N N K H
X E A H Y D E M W X M A E O O
B E U C I L O B M Y S R X S S
D G O S B E B R A H Q I O R T

ATONEMENT	DEATH	FATHER
HOLY GHOST	JESUS	MEMBER
REMISSION OF SINS	RESURRECTION	SON
SYMBOLIC		

The Atonement of Jesus Christ

```
F O R G I V E N E S S D S R L
R L V E D O A V F H E I U R Q
L Y S E P E W Y O I Z S F T N
F Y P M E E T D D E E S F Q V
F C J F H D N Q M W V R E M O
O C H C P N Z T M D D O R M E
E L J H V S P T A V D U E Y I
T B G B U P N V Y M Q D N U
P U B O F L B I R B C X U O X
B O A O I A K P S R R E M M Y
F B J U P S R D O D J K Z K D
S T O T E G K Y S Z M B Q S Y
B S I N V U C J S U S E J O W
M S L X O F I J X G L R L N F
M U U N L F B N Y M Z R X P U
```

BAPTISM   DIED   FORGIVENESS
JESUS   LOVE   REPENTANCE
SINS   SUFFERED

We Become Members of the Church

```
Y  I  F  S  R  L  Q  F  Z  T  C  I  W  A  I
K  R  N  X  N  I  H  T  S  N  H  G  C  H  Y
S  P  A  G  M  L  B  I  Y  E  U  Y  H  D  R
L  Z  H  N  J  Z  W  O  B  M  R  W  U  M  C
Q  X  O  M  O  A  K  I  S  A  C  R  R  M  K
Z  T  I  T  H  I  N  G  S  R  H  T  C  V  S
F  A  P  X  D  M  S  R  Q  C  M  M  H  A  S
O  E  C  L  E  T  O  S  W  A  E  M  E  C  I
Z  H  C  M  F  B  X  O  I  S  E  S  T  B  C
Q  V  B  A  H  T  M  C  Q  M  T  R  Y  H  N
B  E  S  G  L  K  E  I  R  O  I  Y  P  O  H
R  N  I  H  T  L  T  P  N  T  N  Z  M  L  N
I  E  O  W  T  S  I  R  H  C  G  U  S  E  J
N  I  P  Y  S  O  F  N  L  F  S  P  G  F  Z
N  H  W  Z  W  H  D  W  G  O  T  J  I  S  P
```

CALLING	CHURCH	CHURCH MEETINGS
JESUS CHRIST	MEMBER	MISSIONARY
NEIGHBORS	SACRAMENT	TITHING

Obeying God's Commandments

```
V W N I P D C P H X P Y T H M
O I A H E L I S Q H V Z E P D
J L K R K S A V Z Z R A C Z R
E S W K R I J I X E V Z D R B
L D O Z S P A G T E H D D E Y
P E G F P C M A N S I H U F R
M U V X O O T L Q D E V M V W
A M Z G D A Y R E U K L G W X
X S M G W F E C N E I D E B O
E G N C A J E S U S M W J C K
T I M T L R R P P D Y H J Q D
K W H N O O J Z N O V H U U L
U E N W J T T H F D A N P Y V
R M Y V Z A M Q H B U R N M E
U S R P Y L C Q A S F B U R Q
```

CELESTIAL	CTR	EXAMPLE
HEAVENLY FATHER	JESUS	KINGDOM
OBEDIENCE		

The Holy Ghost

ACROSS

2. WE RECEIVE THE HOLY GHOST BY THE LAYING _____ OF HANDS.

3. THE HOLY GHOST HELPS US CHOOSE THE _____.

4. WHEN _____ WAS BAPTIZED THE HOLY GHOST CAME IN THE FORM OF A DOVE.

6. THE HOLY GHOST HELPS US BE _____ TO OTHERS.

DOWN

1. THE HOLY GHOST _____ US IN TIMES OF NEED.

5. THE HOLY GHOST IS A _____ THAT GUIDES US.

The Holy Ghost

```
S  T  W  R  Z  B  I  Y  Q  D  I  H  S  R  Z
T  I  I  A  Q  X  B  L  U  J  B  N  E  Q  Y
I  L  L  R  V  Q  X  S  J  N  B  C  D  Y  P
L  T  L  P  I  S  D  B  Q  D  L  V  I  T  X
L  G  J  I  S  P  F  N  K  H  D  O  U  Z  S
S  T  H  H  F  V  S  I  G  I  F  T  G  K  E
M  G  D  K  R  S  N  S  T  R  O  F  M  O  C
A  B  Y  E  W  D  W  C  F  L  H  L  Q  E  K
L  A  Y  I  N  G  O  N  O  F  H  A  N  D  S
L  O  E  E  F  R  D  X  A  T  C  F  G  T  X
V  I  S  Q  N  F  U  O  U  J  T  F  M  H  I
O  S  G  A  C  V  J  R  V  A  R  B  H  D  P
I  C  D  D  J  S  T  S  A  E  A  C  U  J  L
C  Z  C  Y  S  H  Y  I  U  P  R  O  B  C  Q
E  H  F  V  A  W  S  W  M  Z  A  D  K  L  K
```

COMFORTS	CTR	DOVE
GIFT	GUIDES	KINDNESS
LAYING ON OF HANDS	SPIRIT	STILL SMALL VOICE
TRUTH		

Baptism by Immersion

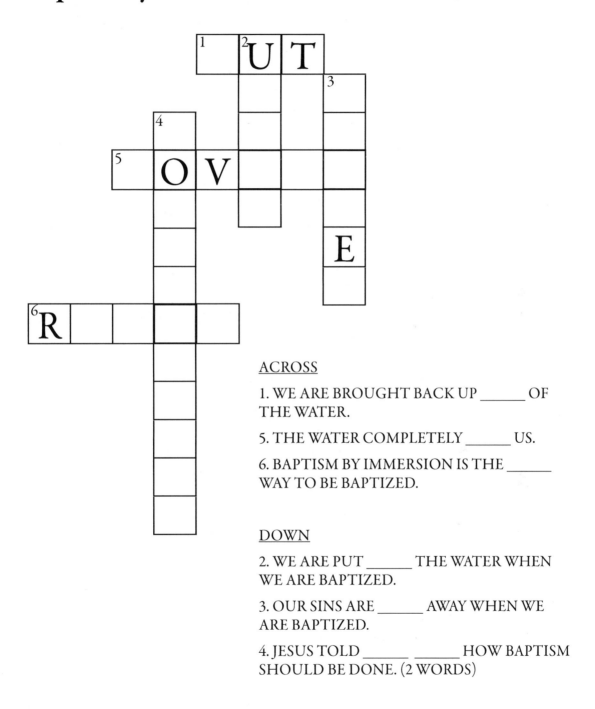

ACROSS

1. WE ARE BROUGHT BACK UP _____ OF THE WATER.

5. THE WATER COMPLETELY _____ US.

6. BAPTISM BY IMMERSION IS THE _____ WAY TO BE BAPTIZED.

DOWN

2. WE ARE PUT _____ THE WATER WHEN WE ARE BAPTIZED.

3. OUR SINS ARE _____ AWAY WHEN WE ARE BAPTIZED.

4. JESUS TOLD _____ _____ HOW BAPTISM SHOULD BE DONE. (2 WORDS)

Baptism by Immersion

```
C O R K V O U G C B X S Q H L
H Z E P N L Q U V O D E T K K
H B T A C Z C Y K W R I I V D
U F A F C V U U Y F M R J J L
U H W U B U B H J S P Q E U H
W B R A C Z G D H R A K V C Z
N F E U E T J P J A K J R U T
G V D Q F N E R E J I M E B E
H Y N K I S M J S H Q B O Y Z
M I U C O R B O U O X T S Y I
U X T J U C C M S P Z N B Q A
M I U W A S H E D A W A Y L Y
Y P P A I L F B U O N K J O V
U E F W B N Z F E A M G V Y Z
D J D J F M V I P V U R W G A
```

CORRECT   JESUS   JOSEPH SMITH
PUT UNDER WATER   WASHED AWAY

Our Baptismal Covenants

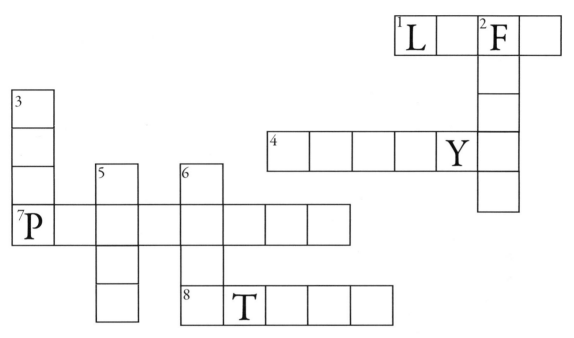

ACROSS

1. HEAVENLY FATHER COVENANTS WITH US TO GIVE US ETERNAL _____.

4. WE COVENANT TO _____ REMEMBER HIM.

7. COVENANTS ARE SACRED _____.

8. WE COVENANT TO _____ AS A WITNESS OF CHRIST AND HIS CHURCH.

DOWN

2. HEAVENLY FATHER COVENANTS WITH US TO COME FORTH ON THE MORNING OF THE _____ RESURRECTION.

3. WE COVENANT TO SERVE HIM AND _____ HIS COMMANDMENTS.

5. HEAVENLY FATHER COVENANTS WITH US TO GIVE US THE GUIDANCE OF THE _____ GHOST.

6. HEAVENLY FATHER COVENANTS WITH US TO FORGIVE OUR _____.

Our Baptismal Covenants

```
N E N S E S C Z E C H E M C U
O U T V T H A C P O S I M O Q
I Y U E U N I C L K H X S V G
T V S R R V E Y R R U K S E E
C I C B R N G M E E J D E N F
E H K E L H A B D T D Y N A M
R U S A O B M L H N J G T N E
R M T S V E H I L L A F I T M
U V T T M E T S R I F M W S B
S E K E S I M O R P F G M N E
E B R J W K N A C R F E L O R
R B U R D E N S N D C P U F C
F O R G I V E N E S S B M Z B
I L F R D P I O W M I P L J N
C H B F Y D P K G V T H Q V K
```

BURDENS   CHURCH   COMMANDMENTS
COVENANTS   ETERNAL LIFE   FIRST
FORGIVENESS   HIS NAME   HOLY GHOST
MEMBER   PROMISE   REMEMBER HIM
RESURRECTION   SACRED   SERVICE
                   WITNESS

Baptism Day

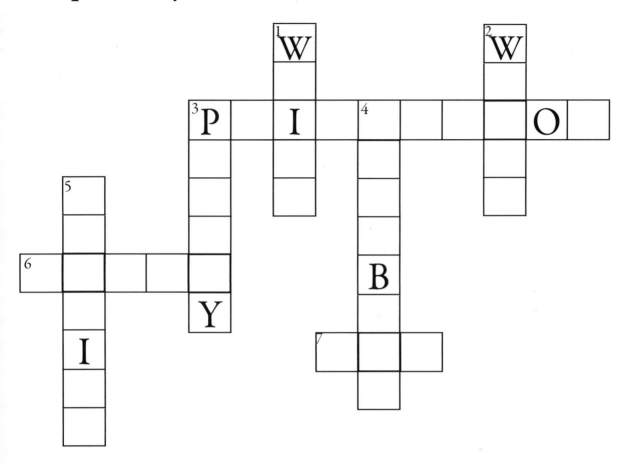

ACROSS

2. WHEN WE TURN EIGHT, WE KNOW RIGHT FROM _____.

3. SOMEONE WITH THE PROPER _____ AUTHORITY WILL BAPTIZE US.

6. WHEN WE TURN _____ YEARS OLD WE WILL BE BAPTIZED.

7. SOMETHING THAT IS PURE IS FREE FROM _____.

DOWN

1. WE WEAR THE COLOR _____ WHEN WE ARE BAPTIZED.

3. WHITE SYMBOLIZES _____.

4. WHITE IS _____ OF SOMETHING WHICH MEANS TO STAND FOR SOMETHING ELSE.

5. AFTER WE ARE BAPTIZED OUR _____ ARE PURE.

We Wear White for Our Baptism

```
N A V M K J W A E O K Q O F G
U J E L I M H Y C R W P X C D
J Y B D W G I B U J W L H G D
R L E H W L T V Z J N H P R J
V I F M S E R V J L T N B S
K Z F T V E K J Z F A I D S A
Y V R G H W L Q F D S D M D B
C G A D Z O G E A M L C J J S
L S H E T L H H O I A X U A W
X G P K K F T R A N H S D R R
E Z K I W N F H X M X X W H O
V T D X R E H A O D I X Y Y L
I U N N E I U J X C C O K U T
U L Y R Z M T M Q U R J X K R
V E F P U R I T Y Y J F X E I
```

FREE FROM SIN   PURITY

WHITE   SPIRIT

Preparing for Baptism

ACROSS

4. WE SHOULD _____ FOR OUR BAPTISM.

5. WE CAN ALSO _____ BEFORE OUR BAPTISM, WHICH MEANS GOING WITHOUT FOOD OR DRINK FOR TWO MEALS.

DOWN

1. TO PREPARE MEANS TO GET _____ FOR SOMETHING.

2. WE SHOULD ALWAYS ATTEND CHURCH _____.

3. WE SHOULD _____ THE SCRIPTURES TO HELP US PREPARE.

4. WE SHOULD _____ TO HEAVENLY FATHER TO HELP US PREPARE.

Preparing for Baptism

```
S  F  T  N  G  P  Y  D  M  A  V  V  K  F  S
C  E  A  U  I  X  A  E  N  Y  T  F  U  F  N
R  G  U  S  V  D  E  X  K  E  S  Z  H  Y  H
I  W  E  A  T  T  I  I  E  Z  T  R  T  H  T
P  V  N  I  I  Y  X  U  C  C  F  T  S  C  E
T  L  P  N  P  R  A  Y  Q  J  F  P  A  R  D
U  V  G  E  R  A  P  E  R  P  M  E  G  U  B
R  S  F  Z  F  I  G  Q  D  A  Y  Y  M  H  E
E  N  T  I  W  C  I  S  O  K  D  N  I  C  M
S  Q  Z  M  P  S  V  E  C  A  X  P  C  V  J
L  E  H  O  O  Z  N  Z  E  Z  W  Q  G  J  B
G  K  L  V  I  F  E  R  K  I  D  S  T  M  J
G  S  I  Y  E  I  S  J  O  Q  R  H  Y  K  U
P  D  M  X  T  P  W  V  B  R  Q  K  R  P  S
A  O  C  A  X  R  V  X  E  N  V  S  T  Y  B
```

ATTEND	CHURCH	FAST
MEETINGS	PRAY	PREPARE
READY	SCRIPTURES	

Prayer

ACROSS

2. WHEN WE PRAY, WE CAN DISCUSS OUR _____ WITH HEAVENLY FATHER.

4. WE SHOULD EXPRESS _____ TO HEAVENLY FATHER WHEN WE PRAY.

DOWN

1. PRAYER KEEPS US _____ TO HEAVENLY FATHER.

2. WE CAN _____ TO HEAVENLY FATHER TO HELP US PREPARE FOR BAPTISM.

3. WE SHOULD BE _____ WHEN WE PRAY.

5. WHEN WE ARE SINCERE, WE ARE TRUTHFUL AND _____ IN WHAT WE SAY.

Prayer

```
H E V Q T Z S W R Q M V S F S
E A U G H L E I N N M X B D S
R E H T A F Y L N E V A E H U
C W B S N U N Y N C Y A R P C
H Y N T K Z S S P N E C N C S
O O N H S Q N M G J V R A T I
C I V U X I O M E F I D E G D
T M K Q P J X V X L X H K N K
F T S C G L S S E D B S J I T
U J S U T R M T F R S O K E C
Q I P H E C V T T C A N R R T
X P L W L S I M H Z S F Z P L
N F S O Y H X Y B X Z M I P M
I N S W Z T I U U F H X V E
A E P Y E E X P R E S S B M U
```

ANSWERS   CLOSE   DISCUSS

EXPRESS   HEAVENLY FATHER   PRAY

PROBLEMS   SINCERE   THANKS

Attending Church Meetings

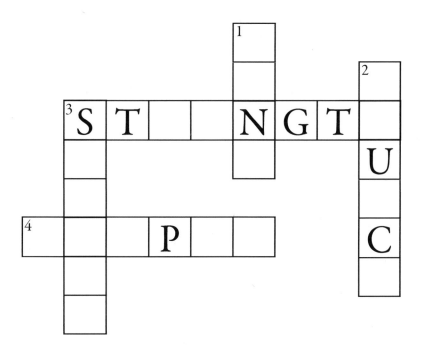

DOWN

1. WE SHOULD _____, PONDER, AND PRAY WHEN WE ARE AT CHURCH.

2. IT IS IMPORTANT TO ATTEND _____ MEETINGS.

3. ATTENDING OUR CHURCH MEETINGS MAKES OUR TESTIMONIES _____.

ACROSS

3. WE ATTEND CHURCH MEETINGS TO GAIN SPIRITUAL _____.

4. WHEN WE ATTEND OUR CHURCH MEETINGS, WE LEARN MORE ABOUT THE _____.

Attending Church Meetings

```
T Y D G K F X M I V G F R U L
K E Z E Q T F T M L R H E B Y
W A S H T G N E R T S L V N J
Y D S T T L E P O Y H W E Z Q
M E N O I T E R K S C H R Q G
E G B E I M A A X I R I E G N
V A Q N T H O W R W U P N I K
Q G G K A T N N P N H P C L O
O S U O K F A P Y A C J E I O
O R S M X B Y Z Y I Y P P I Q
S P I R I T U A L A S U U M A
I B N U S X Y A W O E T C N T
Q X W P I R E H G V S Y G J A
P E H K N C R C O O Z I R Z R
P B H P G R Q P O N D E R N S
```

ATTEND	CHURCH	GOSPEL
LEARN	MEETINGS	PONDER
REVERENCE	SING	SPIRITUAL
STRENGTH	TESTIMONY	

Reading the Scriptures

```
R  P  G  Q  O  S  X  W  D  F  X  Q  A  J  H
C  Y  X  S  A  V  L  E  Y  P  Y  L  A  W  R
O  U  N  H  O  R  K  Z  M  C  U  G  S  N  M
Q  K  Z  P  W  H  W  L  B  T  T  Q  L  X  O
N  C  J  F  T  B  U  E  G  Q  B  L  H  B  D
S  M  U  Z  D  E  E  T  N  Y  C  J  K  Y  N
R  E  H  T  A  F  Y  L  N  E  V  A  E  H  A
W  D  R  D  V  C  F  O  B  B  V  V  Q  C  T
N  N  U  U  K  S  M  T  W  X  U  S  X  F  S
G  L  Q  M  T  I  P  S  Z  Q  X  M  E  S  R
O  A  K  E  T  P  M  I  J  H  E  E  B  O  E
M  O  G  S  C  V  I  V  R  M  L  R  F  W  D
O  Y  E  G  D  H  V  R  V  I  T  E  L  K  N
W  T  L  A  X  I  S  S  C  S  T  A  L  Z  U
C  Z  H  S  T  R  O  N  G  S  N  D  P  M  I
```

FEEL   HEAVENLY FATHER   READ
SCRIPTURES   SPIRIT   STRONG
TESTIMONY   UNDERSTAND

Fasting

```
P O T H E R S T O S S W B H P
L A O A R I K E G L N S E N I
E Q Q V X F P N R E G A H R H
H Y L P V O I C T N V B C L S
L T L U R S E V L E S R U O R
A U A L S A O G N Z M D N G O
I N X E A Y Y L N Z T J I X W
C X L E C U Y D V I V M W S V
E B D O O F T U O H T I W O G
P P C S A G Y I Y A B S X P C
S E V T N E G B R J J T A T W
G G H O E K B A X I Z X D F Y
A E R O Z N H Y J S P Y R O I
R T T J L G P N D R X S V R C
S U K N O W L E D G E D C Z Y
```

BLESSINGS   FASTING   GO WITHOUT FOOD
HEAVENLY FATHER   KNOWLEDGE   OTHERS
OURSELVES   PRAY   SPECIAL HELP
SPIRITUALLY   STRONG   WORSHIP

Reading the Scriptures and Fasting

ACROSS

3. READING THE SCRIPTURES HELPS US UNDERSTAND WHAT HEAVENLY _____ WANTS US TO DO.

4. FASTING MEANS TO GO WITHOUT _____ OR DRINK FOR TWO MEALS.

5. WHEN WE FAST WE CAN ASK HEAVENLY FATHER FOR SPECIAL HELP, KNOWLEDGE, OR _____.

9. WE CAN FAST FOR OURSELVES AND _____.

DOWN

1. FASTING MAKES US SPIRITUALLY _____.

2. WE SHOULD _____ THE SCRIPTURES TO HELP US PREPARE FOR BAPTISM.

6. FASTING SHOWS HEAVENLY FATHER OUR OBEDIENCE AND _____.

7. WHEN WE READ THE SCRIPTURES, IT HELPS US FEEL THE _____.

About Baptism

```
S  S  X  J  Q  N  W  E  B  P  E  W  J  A  Y
A  F  A  K  I  M  V  A  D  L  H  E  H  K  R
C  O  M  C  P  W  P  O  B  I  C  S  L  X  S
R  I  O  E  R  T  K  I  N  X  Q  A  Q  F  U
I  B  E  U  I  A  S  E  K  A  T  S  I  M  S
F  K  F  Z  T  N  M  U  R  Z  N  T  V  X  E
I  R  E  S  O  N  E  E  T  Y  U  I  B  W  J
C  D  M  P  X  P  E  Q  N  N  N  F  Y  M  X
E  Z  S  S  X  S  X  P  O  T  Z  X  G  S  C
D  E  W  C  L  U  D  W  E  S  P  N  Y  F  G
R  G  W  H  Q  I  B  U  A  R  P  D  A  M  K
N  O  S  C  L  Z  C  O  V  E  N  A  N  T  S
D  C  Z  C  A  B  L  X  D  I  D  S  K  Q  B
L  Y  D  G  C  M  L  B  T  O  G  T  O  P  X
O  B  U  N  P  U  I  Y  L  C  Z  K  T  F  X
```

BAPTIZED   COVENANTS   JESUS
KEEP   MISTAKES   REPENT
RESPONSIBLE   SACRAMENT   SACRIFICE

After We Are Baptized

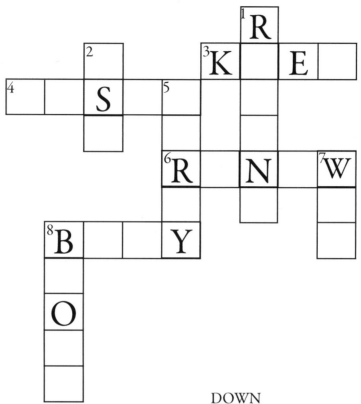

ACROSS

3. WE MUST _____ OUR COVENANTS AFTER WE ARE BAPTIZED.

4. BECAUSE OF THE SACRIFICE _____ MADE FOR US, WE CAN BE FORGIVEN OF OUR SINS.

6. WHEN WE PARTAKE OF THE SACRAMENT, WE _____ OUR COVENANTS WE MADE DURING BAPTISM.

8. THE BREAD HELPS US REMEMBER THE _____ OF JESUS.

DOWN

1. AFTER WE ARE BAPTIZED WE ARE RESPONSIBLE FOR OUR MISTAKES AND MUST _____ TO KEEP OURSELVES CLEAN.

2. WHEN WE REPENT WE _____ FORGIVENESS FOR OUR SINS.

5. REPENTING MEANS FEELING _____ FOR WHAT YOU HAVE DONE.

7. PARTAKING OF THE SACRAMENT HELPS US REMEMBER _____ WE WERE BAPTIZED.

8. THE WATER HELPS US REMEMBER THE _____ THAT JESUS WILLINGLY GAVE FOR US.

The Ordinance of the Sacrament

```
B T D A Q N H L S G F R S N H
M A A D P G S W E E E S U S D
S V P I Y S T P T N U Y S B C
T W O T L E N D E P A M E P D
X N K T I H A W T H B B J O P
O G E I N Z N N Q S Y O O V R
G W V M P R E B O D Y L C W R
F P H W A M V D Q O B I W U W
U O W T E R O L F J Y C X X I
R I D N D D C N Z R S N Y F W
U E O E U V N A O V Y F I F C
I T T P T R J L S O J D B L W
A F E A S A C R I F I C E M D
U U W L W P E F I A S Z X A F
Q Z D A E R B Z D P X U X P D
```

ATONEMENT
BODY
SACRAMENT
SACRIFICE
BLOOD
COVENANTS

BAPTIZED
BREAD
JESUS
SYMBOLIC
RENEW
WATER

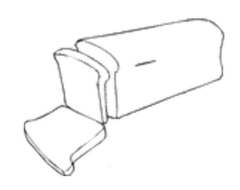